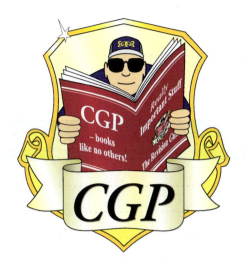

CGP is all you need for Year 1 Maths!

This brilliant CGP Study Book covers everything that pupils need to know for the Year 1 Maths Programme of Study.

It's packed full of clear explanations and helpful examples, all perfectly matched to the National Curriculum. And if that wasn't enough, we've included practice questions for every section — ideal for checking that it's all sunk in.

There are even answers to every single question at the back of the book — put all that together and you're ready for Year 1 Maths success!

What CGP is all about

Our sole aim here at CGP is to produce the highest quality books — carefully written, immaculately presented and dangerously close to being funny.

Then we work our socks off to get them out to you — at the cheapest possible prices.

Contents

About This Book 1

Section One — Number and Place Value

One to Twenty 2
Tens and Ones 3
Counting to 100 4
How Many? 5
Twos, Fives and Tens 6
The Number Line 7
Ordering and Patterns 8
Practice Questions 9

Section Two — Addition and Subtraction

Number Bonds to 10 10
Number Bonds to 20 11
Add, Subtract and Equals Signs 12
Adding 13
Subtracting 14
Adding and Subtracting 15
Practice Questions 16

Section Three — Multiplication and Division

Multiplying 17
Dividing 18
Practice Questions 19

Section Four — Fractions

Halves 20
Quarters 21
Practice Questions 22

Section Five — Measurement

Length and Height 23
Measuring Length and Height 24
Mass 25
Measuring Mass 26
Volume 27
Measuring Volume 28
Money 29
Dates 30
Days 31
Time 32
Measuring Time 33
Practice Questions 34

Section Six — Geometry

Flat (2D) Shapes 35
Solid (3D) Shapes 36
Position 37
Direction and Turns 38
Practice Questions 39

Answers 40
Important Maths Words 43
Index 47

Published by CGP

Editors:
Martha Bozic, Sarah George, Hannah Lawson, Sean McParland, Alison Palin, Caley Simpson.

ISBN: 978 1 78908 918 9

With thanks to Simon Little and Gail Renaud for the proofreading.
With thanks to Jan Greenway for the copyright research.

Images on the cover and throughout the book © Educlips
Clipart from Corel®

£1 coin © iStock.com/LPETTET

Printed by Elanders Ltd, Newcastle upon Tyne.
Based on the classic CGP style created by Richard Parsons.

Text, design, layout and original illustrations © Coordination Group Publications Ltd. (CGP) 2022
All rights reserved.

Photocopying more than one section of this book is not permitted, even if you have a CLA licence.
Extra copies are available from CGP with next day delivery • 0800 1712 712 • www.cgpbooks.co.uk

About This Book

This Book has All the Topics for Year 1

By the end of Year 1, you should be able to do all the maths in this book.

Each page covers a different topic and shows you the maths that you need to know.

This book covers the Attainment Targets for Year 1 of the National Curriculum.

There are also practice questions at the end of each section. These can help you see which topics you really understand and which ones you need to work on.

There are answers to every question at the back of the book.

> There's a matching Question Book for this Study Book.
> It has questions on every topic, plus some practice tests.

There are Learning Objectives for Each Topic

Learning objectives say what you should be able to do.

You can use the tick boxes for ongoing assessment to record which attainment targets have been met. Printable checklists of all the objectives can be found at cgpbooks.co.uk/PrimaryMathsLO or by scanning this QR code.

Use the tick boxes to show how happy you feel.

Tick here if you need a bit more practice.

Tick here if you're really struggling.

Tick here if you can do all the maths on the page.

"I can read and write numbers up to 20."

Section One — Number and Place Value

One to Twenty

Numbers and Words

Learn all these numbers.

 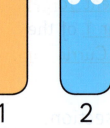      

1 One   2 Two   3 Three   4 Four   5 Five   6 Six   7 Seven   8 Eight

  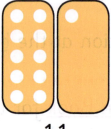  

9 Nine   10 Ten   11 Eleven   12 Twelve   13 Thirteen

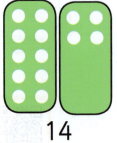 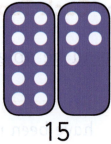 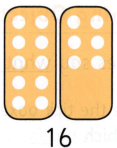 

14 Fourteen   15 Fifteen   16 Sixteen   17 Seventeen

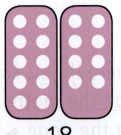 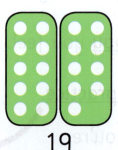   

18 Eighteen   19 Nineteen   20 Twenty

"I can read and write numbers up to 20."

Tens and Ones

Small Numbers are Made of Ones

3 ones

5 ones

Bigger Numbers are Made of Tens and Ones

14 is made up of 1 group of ten and 4 ones.

Tens	Ones
🪐	🪐🪐🪐🪐

23 is made up of 2 groups of ten and 3 ones.

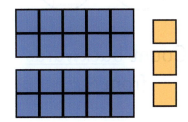

Tens	Ones
🪐🪐	🪐🪐🪐

"I can show numbers using tens and ones."

Section One — Number and Place Value

Counting to 100

Numbers From 0 to 100

Read across each line of numbers.

0	1	2	3	4	5	6	7	8	9	10
	11	12	13	14	15	16	17	18	19	20
	21	22	23	24	25	26	27	28	29	30
	31	32	33	34	35	36	37	38	39	40
	41	42	43	44	45	46	47	48	49	50
	51	52	53	54	55	56	57	58	59	60
	61	62	63	64	65	66	67	68	69	70
	71	72	73	74	75	76	77	78	79	80
	81	82	83	84	85	86	87	88	89	90
	91	92	93	94	95	96	97	98	99	100

101 comes after 100

Counting Forwards and Backwards

Count forwards from 24.

24 → 25 → 26 → 27

Bingo!

Count backwards from 92.

89 ← 90 ← 91 ← 92

"I can read and write numbers to 100.
I can count to 100 forwards and backwards."

Section One — Number and Place Value

How Many?

More or Less

Count how many things you have in each group.

There are **4** pineapples.   There are **3** pears.

There are more pineapples than pears.   4 is more than 3.

There are fewer pears than pineapples.   3 is less than 4.

Most and Least

Compare the big squares below.

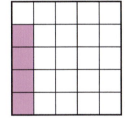 This big square is the least shaded. 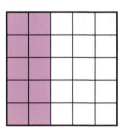 This big square is the most shaded.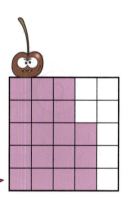

Things that are the Same are Equal

There is an equal amount of fruit in each group.

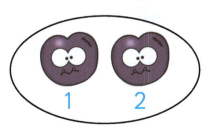 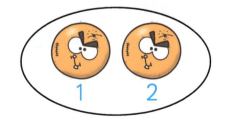 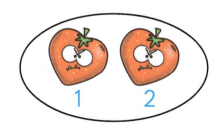

"I can compare numbers of objects by counting."

Section One — Number and Place Value

Twos, Fives and Tens

Counting in Twos

Count on in twos from 0.

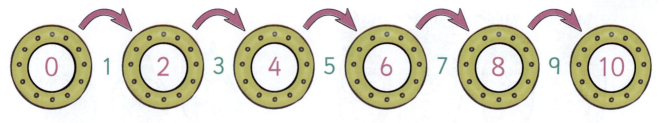

Even numbers end in a 0, 2, 4, 6 or 8.
Odd numbers end in a 1, 3, 5, 7 or 9.

Counting in Fives

Now count on in fives from 0.

Counting in Tens

And now count on in tens from 0.

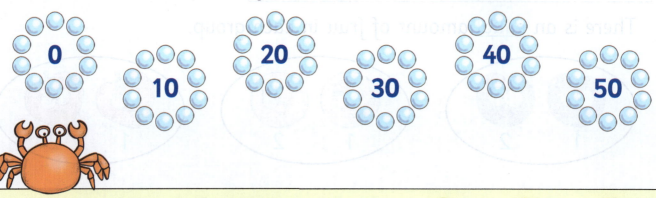

"I can count in twos, fives and tens."

Section One — Number and Place Value

The Number Line

The Number Line Is Very Long

The numbers get bigger as you go right.

0 1 2 3 4 5 6 7 8 9 10 11 12

They get smaller as you go left.

4 is less than 7

7 is more than 4

Find One More Or One Less

Find one more than 5.
Move one space to the right.

Find one less than 8.
Move one space to the left.

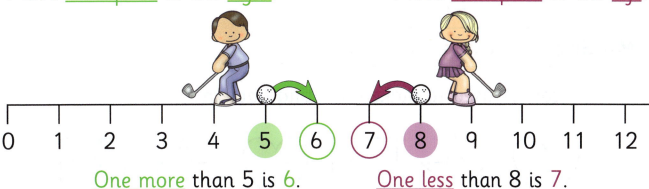

One more than 5 is 6.

One less than 8 is 7.

To find two more or two less than a number, move two spaces.

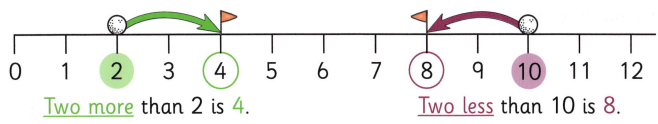

Two more than 2 is 4.

Two less than 10 is 8.

"I can use numbers on a number line.
I can find one more and one less than a number."

Section One — Number and Place Value

Ordering and Patterns

Finishing First

The winner comes first. Then there's second and third place.

1st
First

2nd
Second

3rd
Third

After 3rd comes 4th (fourth), 5th (fifth), 6th (sixth), 7th (seventh) and 8th (eighth).

Making Repeating Patterns

Shapes can be used to make repeating patterns.

And so can numbers.

1 3 5 1 3 5

"I can order objects and recognise patterns."

Section One — Number and Place Value

Practice Questions

1 Write each word as a number.

    a) Seven   b) Twelve   c) Eighteen

2 Which pile has the most sweets in it?

A   B    C

3 What is one less than 19?
Use the number line to help you.

10   11   12   13   14   15   16   17   18   19   20

4 What are the missing numbers?

    a) 0   5   ?   15   20   b) 50   40   30   ?   10

5 What is the next number in the pattern?

4   7   6   4   7   ?

6 The table on the right shows the number 16. Make a similar table for the number 24.

Tens	Ones
●	●●● ●●●

Section One — Number and Place Value

Section Two — Addition and Subtraction

Number Bonds to 10

Pairs of Numbers That Make **10**

These are the number bonds to 10.

0 + 10 = 10

10 − 0 = 10

1 + 9 = 10

10 − 1 = 9

2 + 8 = 10

10 − 2 = 8

3 + 7 = 10

10 − 3 = 7

4 + 6 = 10

10 − 4 = 6

5 + 5 = 10

10 − 5 = 5

Find number bonds to other numbers.
Here are the pairs that make 6:
0 + 6   1 + 5   2 + 4   3 + 3

"I can use number bonds up to 10."

Number Bonds to 20

Pairs of Numbers That Make **20**

These are some number bonds to 20.

0 + 20 = 20
20 − 0 = 20

1 + 19 = 20
20 − 1 = 19

2 + 18 = 20
20 − 2 = 18

3 + 17 = 20
20 − 3 = 17

4 + 16 = 20
20 − 4 = 16

And some more.

5 + 15 = 20	6 + 14 = 20
7 + 13 = 20	8 + 12 = 20
9 + 11 = 20	10 + 10 = 20

Here are some number bonds to 13:

0 + 13
2 + 11
4 + 9
7 + 6

"I can use number bonds up to 20."

Section Two — Addition and Subtraction

Add, Subtract and Equals Signs

+ Means Add

+ means put numbers together.

= means equals.
It tells you the total.

1 + 2 = 3

1 add 2 equals 3

− Means Subtract

− means take away a number.

4 − 1 = 3

4 subtract 1 equals 3

"I can write statements using addition (+), subtraction (−) and equals (=) signs."

Section Two — Addition and Subtraction

Adding

Add By Counting

What is 4 + 2?

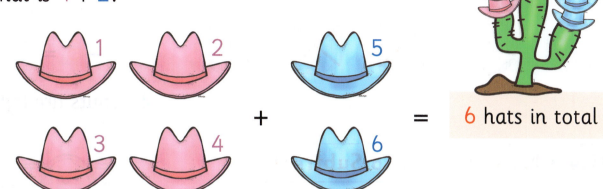

4 + 2 = 6

Use a Number Line To Add

To add one, go one step to the right (→).

What is 4 + 1?

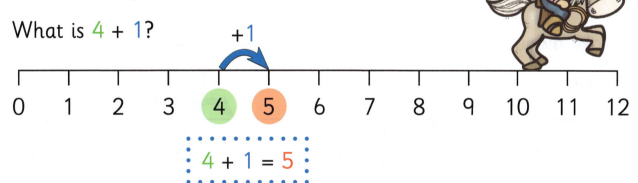

4 + 1 = 5

To add more than one, count right (→) in steps.

What is 14 + 5?

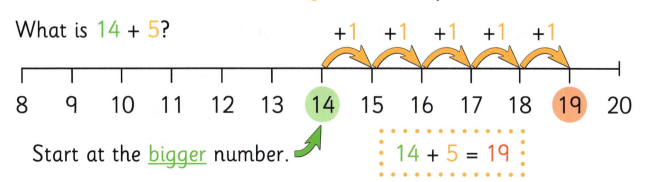

Start at the bigger number.   14 + 5 = 19

"I can add 1-digit and 2-digit numbers up to 20."

Section Two — Addition and Subtraction

Subtracting

Subtract By Counting

What is 5 − 3?

 1   2   3   4   5

5 − 3 = 2

2 donuts are left.

Use a Number Line To Subtract

To take away <u>one</u>, go <u>one step</u> to the <u>left</u> (←).

What is 6 − 1?

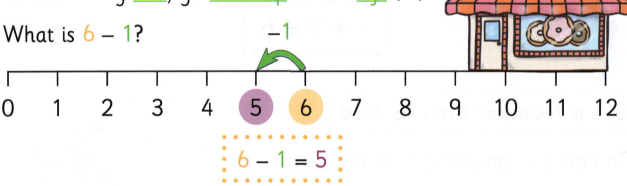

6 − 1 = 5

To take away <u>more than one</u>, count <u>left</u> (←) in steps.

What is 12 − 4?

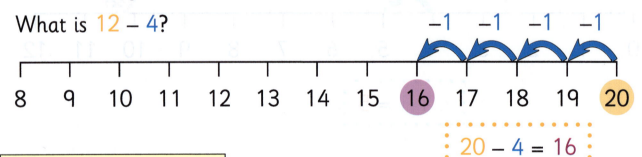

20 − 4 = 16

Find the Difference

<u>Difference</u> means the <u>gap</u> between numbers.

6
4

The <u>difference between</u> 6 and 4 is 2.

6 − 4 = 2

"I can subtract 1-digit and 2-digit numbers up to 20."

Section Two — Addition and Subtraction

Adding and Subtracting

Add and Subtract To Solve Problems

There are <u>4 yellow ducks</u> and <u>5 brown ducks</u> at the park.
How many ducks are there in total?

$$4 + 5 = 9$$

There are 9 ducks in <u>total</u>.

> Addition is the <u>opposite</u> of subtraction.

All of the <u>brown ducks</u> swim away.
How many ducks are left at the park?

$$9 - 5 = 4$$

There are 4 ducks <u>left</u> at the park.

Nothing Happens When You Use Zero

When you <u>add</u> or <u>subtract</u> zero,
the number will always <u>stay the same</u>.

$$2 + 0 = 2 \qquad 3 - 0 = 3$$

"I can solve number problems by adding and subtracting."

Practice Questions

1 Which symbols +, − or = go in the gaps below?

2 What is the difference between the number of bicycles and the number of cars?

3 Use number bonds to find the missing numbers below.

a) 11 + ? = 20

b) 20 − ? = 17

4 Give two pairs of numbers that add up to 8.

5 Find the answer to 13 + 4 using this number line.

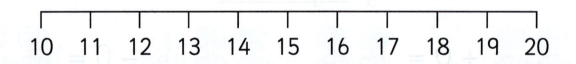

6 April has 7 hair bands. She loses 2 of them.

How many hair bands does April have left?

Section Two — Addition and Subtraction

Section Three — Multiplication and Division

Multiplying

Counting In Equal Groups

How many birds are there?

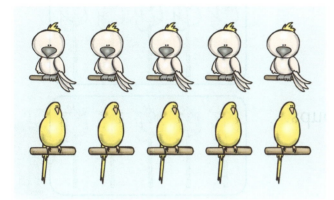

There are 2 groups of 5 birds.

5 + 5 = 10 birds

Write it as 2 × 5 = 10
2 times 5 = 10

This is called multiplying.
2 multiplied by 5 = 10

Use a Number Line

Count right (→) in groups of 5.

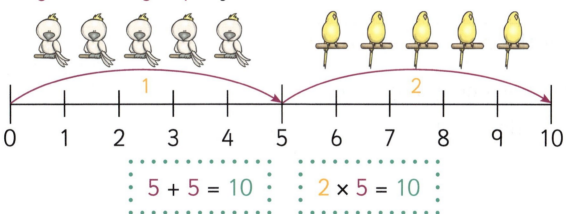

5 + 5 = 10   2 × 5 = 10

Group Things in Different Ways

2 groups of 4 hamsters

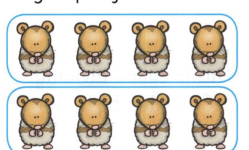

2 × 4 = 8
4 × 2 = 8

4 groups of 2 hamsters

"I can count in equal groups."

Dividing

Sharing In Equal Groups

Share 15 flowers between 3 fairies.

How many flowers does each fairy get?

Share the flowers into 3 equal groups.

Each fairy gets 5 flowers.

Write it as 15 ÷ 3 = 5

Find the Number of Groups

How many groups of 5 are in 20?

Count right (→) in fives from 0 to 20.

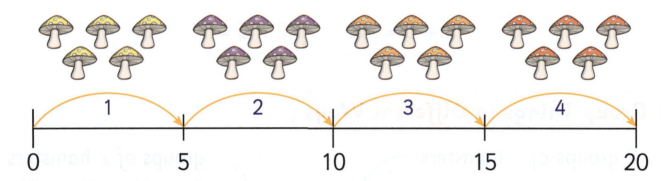

There are 4 groups of 5 in 20.

20 ÷ 5 = 4

This is called dividing.
20 divided by 5 = 4

"I can share a number into groups."

Practice Questions

1 Share the nuts equally between the squirrels. How many nuts does each squirrel get?

2 Copy this number line. Show 6 × 2 on your number line, then find the missing number in 6 × 2 = ⬚.

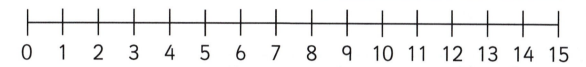

3 How many groups of 3 are in 12? Use the dots to help.

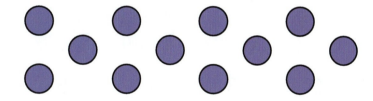

4 Copy and complete the number sentences to show how many carrots there are in total.

a) 2 + ⬚ + 2 + 2 + 2 = ⬚

b) 5 × ⬚ = ⬚

Section Three — Multiplication and Division

Section Four — Fractions

Halves

A Whole has Two Equal Halves

Splitting something into two equal parts makes two halves.

Like this pizza.

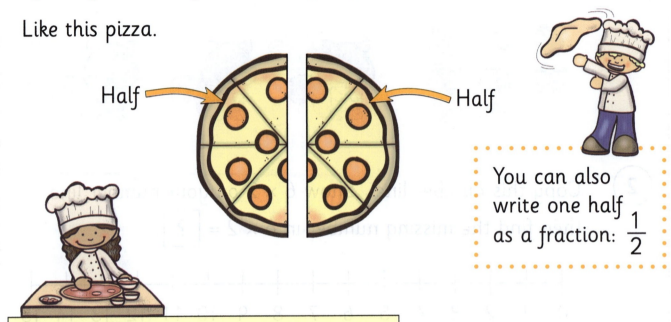

You can also write one half as a fraction: $\frac{1}{2}$

You Can Have Half of a Group Too

There are 6 marbles. Each child has an equal number of marbles.

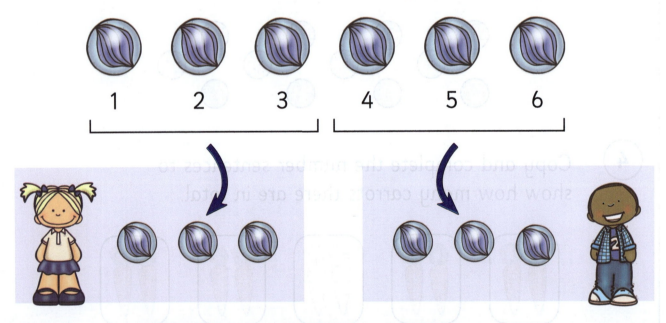

Half of the total number of marbles is 3.
So each child has 3 marbles.

"I can find one half of objects, shapes and quantities."

Quarters

Quarters are Made by Splitting into Four

If you cut something into four equal parts, each part is a quarter.

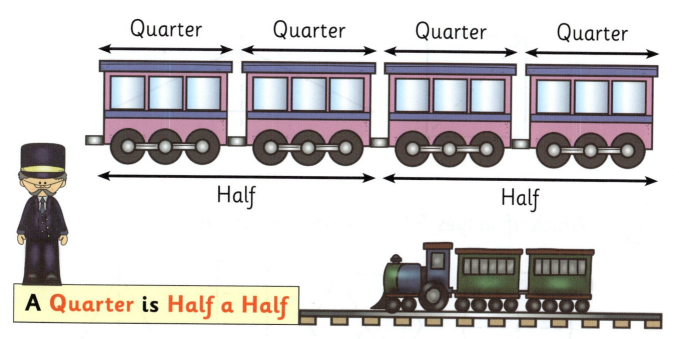

A Quarter is Half a Half

This is how you'd shade a quarter of a shape:

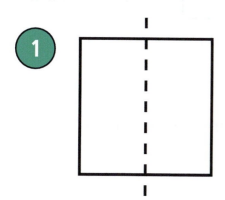

Draw a line in the middle to make two halves.

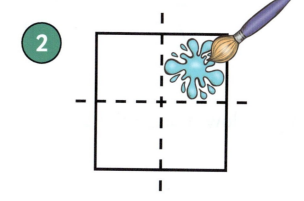

Draw another line to make four quarters. Then shade in one quarter.

Two quarters is the same as one half.

Three quarters is the same as one half and one quarter.

"I can find one quarter of objects, shapes and quantities."

Section Four — Fractions

Practice Questions

1 Copy these shapes onto a piece of paper.
Then shade half of each one.

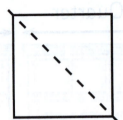 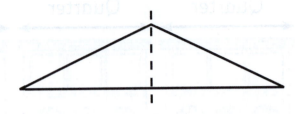

2 Which of shapes A-D have one quarter shaded?

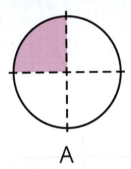 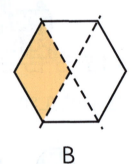  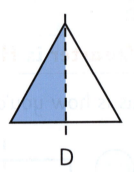

A   B   C   D

3 How many robots are in one quarter of this group?

4 Aisha has 8 balloons. She pops half of them.
How many balloons does she pop?

Section Four — Fractions

Section Five — Measurement

Length and Height

Lengths Can Be Long or Short

Things can be long.

The opposite of long is short.

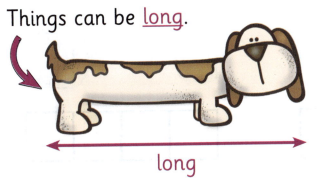

long

short

You can compare lengths.

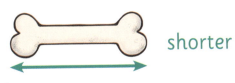

shorter

longer

The rope is double the length of the bone.
The bone is half the length of the rope.

Heights Can Be Tall or Short

Things can be tall.

You can compare heights.

The tree is double the height of the ladder.
The ladder is half the height of the tree.

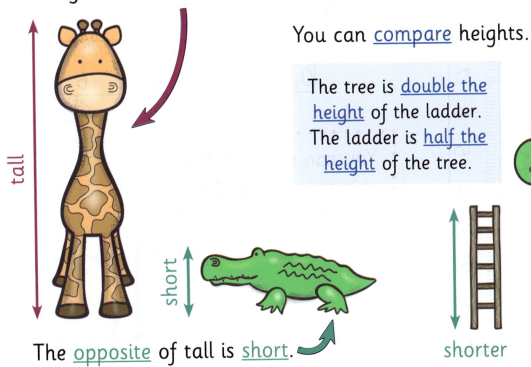

tall

short

shorter

taller

The opposite of tall is short.

"I can compare lengths and heights."

Measuring Length and Height

Measure Length and Height With Blocks

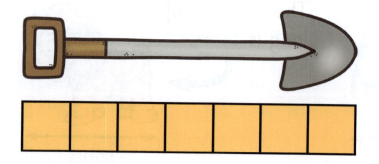

This spade is <u>7 blocks</u> long.

This spade is <u>4 blocks</u> long.

The <u>grey</u> spade is <u>longer</u> than the <u>red</u> spade.

Measure Length and Height in Centimetres (cm)

Use a <u>ruler</u>.

This grass is <u>8 cm</u> tall.

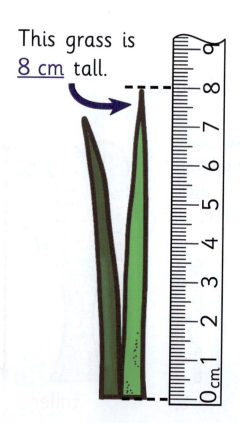

This caterpillar is <u>5 cm</u> long.

You can measure <u>big</u> things in <u>metres (m)</u>.

2 m

"I can measure lengths and heights."

Mass

Things Can Be Heavy or Light

The mass of something is how heavy or light it is.
Mass can be called weight.

An object that weighs a lot is heavy.

A sofa is heavy.

A bath is heavy.

An object that doesn't weigh a lot is light.

A cup is light.

A rubber duck is light.

You Can Compare Masses

Heavier objects weigh more than lighter objects.

A cat is heavier than a sponge.

A sponge is lighter than a cat.

"I can compare how heavy objects are."

Section Five — Measurement

Measuring Mass

Weigh Things to Measure Mass

The crab weighs six blocks.

The seaweed weighs two blocks.

The crab weighs more than the seaweed.

Measure Mass in Grams (g)

Use scales.

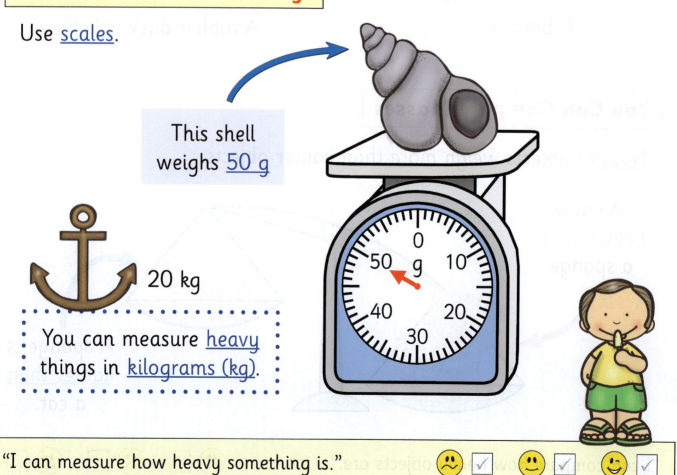

This shell weighs 50 g

20 kg

You can measure heavy things in kilograms (kg).

"I can measure how heavy something is."

Section Five — Measurement

Volume

Things Can Be Empty or Full

This jug is empty.

This jug is full.

You Can Compare Volumes

Volume is how much of something there is.
Look at these two jugs.

How much a container can hold is called its capacity.

This jug is more full. It is less empty.

This jug is more empty. It is less full.

Half Full and Quarter Full

 This jar is a quarter full.

 This jar is half full.

 Half full is the same as half empty.

 More than half full

 Less than half full

 Less than a quarter full

"I can compare how full containers are."

Section Five — Measurement

Measuring Volume

Fill Things to Measure Volume

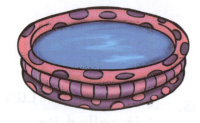

10 buckets fill this paddling pool.   4 buckets fill this fish tank.

The paddling pool holds more than the fish tank.

Measure Volume in Millilitres (ml)

Use a measuring jug or cylinder.

Fill the jar with water.

You can measure big volumes in litres (l).

Pour the water into a measuring jug.

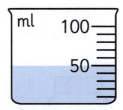

The jar holds 50 millilitres.

"I can measure how full a container is and how much it can hold."

Section Five — Measurement

Money

There are 8 Different Coins

1 penny
1p

2 pence
2p

5 pence
5p

10 pence
10p

20 pence
20p

50 pence
50p

1 pound
£1

2 pounds
£2

1 pound is the same as 100 pence.

Paper Money is Worth More

These are called <u>notes</u>.

20 pounds
£20

10 pounds
£10

5 pounds
£5

"I know the value of different coins and notes."

Section Five — Measurement

Dates

There are 7 Days in a Week

| Monday | Tuesday | Wednesday | Thursday | Friday | Saturday | Sunday |

The order is important.

Days are Grouped into Months

There are 12 months in a year.

January is the first month.

Sometimes February has 29 days.

The month after March is April.

January 31 days	February 28 days	March 31 days	April 30 days
May 31 days	June 30 days	July 31 days	August 31 days
September 30 days	October 31 days	November 30 days	December 31 days

The month before October is September.

There are 365 days in a year.

"I know the days of the week, and how days are arranged into months and years."

Days

Today, Yesterday and Tomorrow

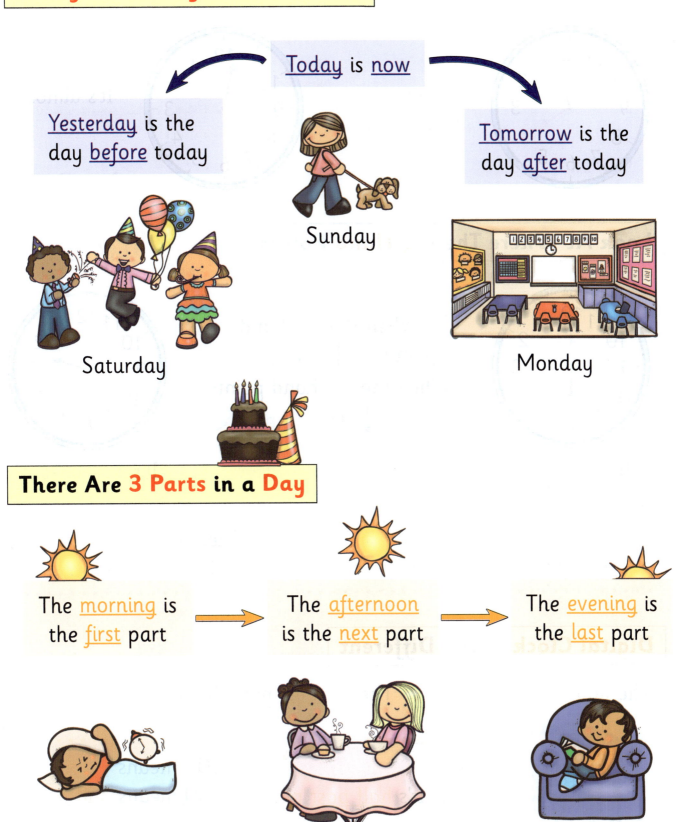

There Are 3 Parts in a Day

The <u>morning</u> is the <u>first</u> part → The <u>afternoon</u> is the <u>next</u> part → The <u>evening</u> is the <u>last</u> part

"I can describe when events happen."

Section Five — Measurement

Time

The Little Hand Shows Hours

It's just after four.

It's almost eleven.

Look At Where The Big Hand Points

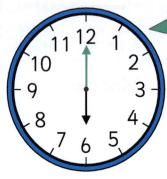

When the big hand points up ↑, it's o'clock.
When the big hand points down ↓, it's half past.

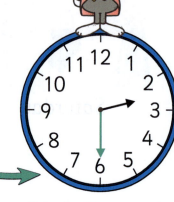

It's 6 o'clock.

It's half past 2.

The big hand shows minutes.

There are 60 minutes in one hour.

There are 30 minutes in half an hour.

Digital Clocks Look Different

The hour   The minutes past the hour

It's half past nine

:00 means o'clock
:30 means half past

"I can tell the time and draw hands on a clock face to show the time."

Section Five — Measurement

Measuring Time

Measure Time in Hours, Minutes and Seconds

seconds → minutes → hours

A bigger time is a longer time.
A smaller time is a shorter time.

Ailsa and Noah went on a bike ride.

Ailsa took 20 minutes.

Ailsa was quicker.

Noah took 28 minutes.

Noah was slower.

Time Can Be Earlier Or Later

A time before another is earlier.

3 o'clock is earlier than 4 o'clock.

A time after another is later.

Half past 1 is later than 1 o'clock.

"I can compare times. I know how to record time in hours, minutes and seconds."

Section Five — Measurement

Practice Questions

1. Decide whether each object is heavy or light.

   a) a pencil   b) a digger   c) a horse

2. Today is Tuesday. Which day was it yesterday?

3. Which coin has the biggest value?

4. Which of the objects below are longer than 7 cm?

   a pin   a TV   an iron   an ant   a bike

5. How many litres of water are in this jug? Is it more or less than half full?

6. Read the time on each clock. Which time is later?

Section Five — Measurement

Section Six — Geometry

Flat (2D) Shapes

Learn these shapes.

Shapes You Need To Know

Rectangle

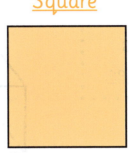

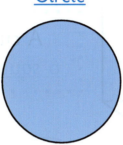
Circle

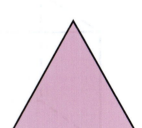
Triangle

All the sides of a square are the same length.

Some Shapes Can Look Different

But they are still the same.

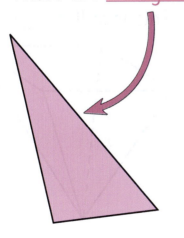

These are triangles too.

These are also rectangles.

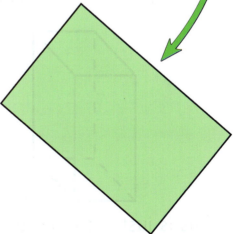

"I can identify and name 2D shapes."

Solid (3D) Shapes

3D shapes are solid.

Learn These Solid Shapes

Cube

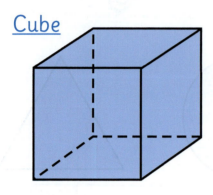

A cube has 6 square faces.

Cuboid

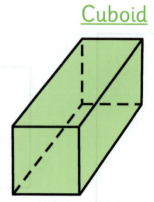

Sphere

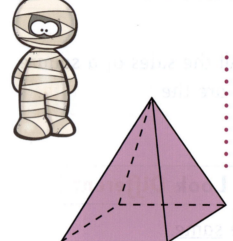

Pyramids can have triangle bases too.

Pyramid

Sometimes They Might Be Upside Down

But they are still the same shape.

This is still a pyramid.

This is just a cuboid on its end.

"I can identify and name 3D shapes."

Position

Say Where Things Are

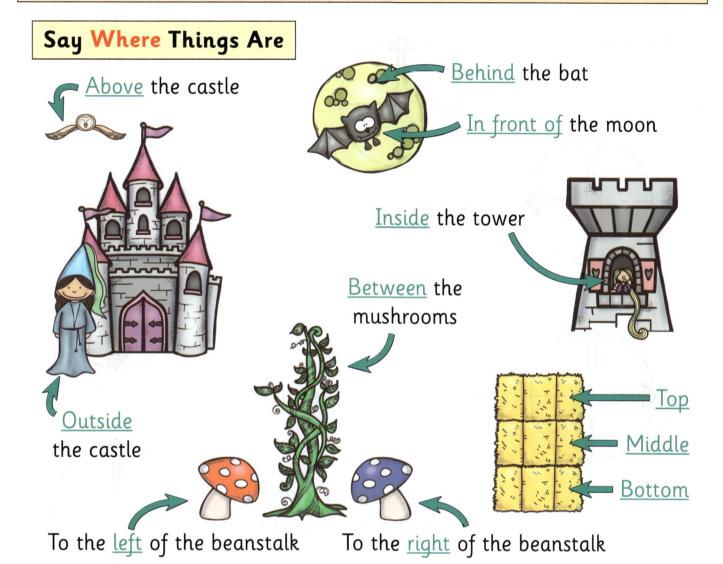

Above the castle

Behind the bat

In front of the moon

Inside the tower

Between the mushrooms

Outside the castle

Top
Middle
Bottom

To the left of the beanstalk

To the right of the beanstalk

Say How Things Move

A van can go backwards

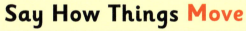

You can go up a ladder

And down

Or forwards

"I can describe where things are and how they are moving."

Section Six — Geometry

Direction and Turns

Making Turns

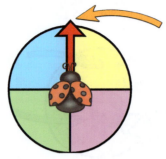 The pointer starts <u>here</u>.

 This is a <u>quarter turn</u>.

Here is a <u>half turn</u>.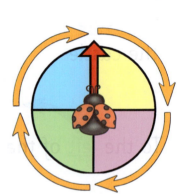

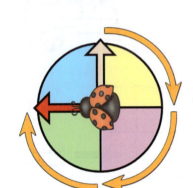 This is a <u>three-quarter</u> turn.

A <u>whole turn</u> you gets you back to where you started.

Clockwise and Anticlockwise

The hands on a clock turn <u>clockwise</u>.

<u>Anticlockwise</u> is the <u>opposite</u> direction.

"I can describe a movement using whole, half, quarter and three-quarter turns."

Section Six — Geometry

Practice Questions

1 Which of these objects are cubes?

  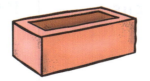 

2 Which direction is each child moving in? Choose from forwards, backwards, up or down.

3 Which picture (1-4) shows this panda after a quarter turn anticlockwise?

  1   2   3   4

4 Use the shapes to answer the questions.

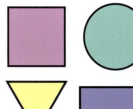

  a) Which shape is above the triangle?

  b) Which shape is to the right of the square?

Section Six — Geometry

Answers

Section One — Number and Place Value

Page 9 — Practice Questions

1) a) **7**

   b) **12**

   c) **18**

2) Pile **B** has the most sweets in it.

3) Find 19 and move one space to the left.
   One less than 19 is **18**.

4) a) 0 5 **10** 15 20

   b) 50 40 30 **20** 10

5) 4 7 6 4 7 6

6) E.g.

Tens	Ones
●●	●●● ●●

Section Two — Addition and Subtraction

Page 16 — Practice Questions

1)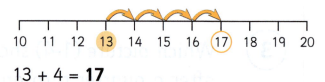

2) There are 8 bicycles and 5 cars.
   8 − 5 = **3**

3) a) 11 + **9** = 20

   b) 20 − **3** = 17

4) Any two from: **0 + 8**
   1 + 7
   2 + 6
   3 + 5
   4 + 4

5) Count four places to the right.

   13 + 4 = **17**

6) April has 7 − 2 = **5** hair bands left.

Answers

Section Three — Multiplication and Division

Page 19 — Practice Questions

1) There are 9 nuts and 3 squirrels.

   Each squirrel gets 3 nuts, so 9 shared by 3 is **3**.

2) Count right in 6 groups of 2, e.g.

   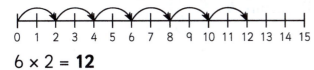

   6 × 2 = **12**

3)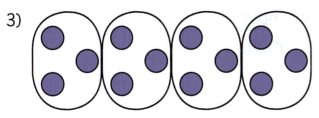

   12 shared into groups of 3 = **4 groups**

4) a) 2 + **2** + 2 + 2 + 2 = **10**

   b) 5 × **2** = **10**

Section Four — Fractions

Page 22 — Practice Questions

1) E.g.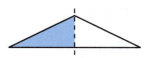

2)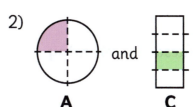

   A and C

3) There are 4 robots in the group. One quarter of 4 robots is **1** robot.

4) 🎈🎈🎈🎈🎈🎈🎈🎈 (first 4 crossed out)

   One half of 8 is 4, so she popped **4 balloons**.

Answers

Section Five — Measurement

Page 34 — Practice Questions

1) a) **Light**
   b) **Heavy**
   c) **Heavy**

2) The day before Tuesday is **Monday**.

3)

4) A **TV**, an **iron** and a **bike** are longer than 7 cm.

5) **4 litres**
   It is **less** than half full.

6) The time on the first clock is **5 o'clock**. The time on the second clock is **half past 4**.
   5 o'clock is later than half past 4.

Section Six — Geometry

Page 39 — Practice Questions

1)  are cubes.

2) up    forwards

    backwards    down

3) Picture **4**:

4) a) **Square**
   b) **Circle**

Important Maths Words

2D	2D is short for two-dimensional. It means flat.
3D	3D is short for three-dimensional. It means solid — something you can pick up.
add	Put together two numbers to find the total. + is the sign for add.
anticlockwise	Turning the opposite way to the hands of a clock.
capacity	How much something can hold. It can be measured in millilitres (ml) or litres (l).
centimetre (cm)	A unit for measuring height or length.
circle	A perfectly round 2D shape.
clockwise	Turning the same way as the hands of a clock.
cube	A 3D shape with 6 square faces.
cuboid	A 3D shape with 6 rectangle faces.
day	A unit of time. There are 7 days in a week — Monday, Tuesday, Wednesday, Thursday, Friday, Saturday and Sunday.

Important Maths Words

divide	Share into equal groups. ÷ is the sign for divide.
equals	The same. = is the sign for equals.
even	A number that ends in 0, 2, 4, 6, or 8.
fraction	A part of something whole. Like a half or a quarter.
gram (g)	A unit for measuring weight or mass.
half	One of two equal parts. It can be written as $\frac{1}{2}$.
height	How tall something is. It can be measured in centimetres (cm) or metres (m).
hour	A unit of time. There are 24 hours in a day.
kilogram (kg)	A unit for measuring weight or mass.
length	How long or short something is. It can be measured in centimetres (cm) or metres (m).
litre (l)	A unit for measuring volume or capacity.
mass	How heavy or light something is. It can be measured in grams (g) or kilograms (kg).

Important Maths Words

metre (m)	A unit for measuring height or length.
millilitre (ml)	A unit for measuring volume or capacity.
minute	A unit of time. There are 60 minutes in an hour.
month	A unit of time. There are 12 months in a year — January, February, March, April, May, June, July, August, September, October, November and December.
multiply	Counting in groups of numbers. × is the sign for multiply.
number line	A line with numbers used for counting.
odd	A number that ends in 1, 3, 5, 7 or 9.
pence (p)	A unit of money. There are 100 pence in a pound. You can get 1p, 2p, 5p, 10p, 20p and 50p coins.
pound (£)	A unit of money. You can get £1 and £2 coins, and £5, £10, £20 and £50 notes.
pyramid	A 3D shape with a flat base and a point at the top.

Important Maths Words

quarter	One of four equal parts. It can be written as $\frac{1}{4}$.
rectangle	A 2D shape with 4 sides.
second	A unit of time. There are 60 seconds in a minute.
sphere	A perfectly round 3D shape.
square	A 2D shape with all four sides the same.
subtract	Take away one number from another. − is the sign for subtract.
total	Everything added together.
triangle	A 2D shape with 3 sides.
volume	How much of something there is. It can be measured in millilitres (ml) or litres (l).
week	A unit of time. There are 7 days in a week.
weight	How heavy or light something is. It can be measured in grams (g) or kilograms (kg).
year	A unit of time. There are 12 months or 365 days in a year.

Index

2D shapes 35
3D shapes 36

A

adding 12, 13, 15
afternoon 31
anticlockwise 38

C

capacity 27
centimetres (cm) 24
circles 35
clocks 32
clockwise 38
coins 29
counting
    4, 5, 13, 14
  in fives 6
  in tens 6
  in twos 6
cubes 36
cuboids 36

D

dates 30
days 30, 31
difference 14
digital clocks 32
direction 38
dividing 18

E

earlier 33
empty 27
equal 5
equals sign (=) 12
evening 31
even numbers 6

F

first place 8
fractions 20, 21
full 27

G

grams (g) 26
grouping 17

H

half full 27
half past 32
half turn 38
halves 20
heavy 25, 26
height 23, 24
hours 32, 33

K

kilograms (kg) 26

L

later 33
least 5
length 23, 24
less than 5
light 25
litres (l) 28
long 23, 24

M

mass 25, 26
measuring 24, 26, 28
measuring jugs 28
metres (m) 24
millilitres (ml) 28
minutes 32, 33
money 29
months 30
more than 5
morning 31
most 5
movement 37
multiplying 17

N

notes 29
number bonds 10, 11
number lines
    7, 13, 14, 17, 18
numbers 2

Index

O
o'clock 32, 33
odd numbers 6
ones 3
ordering 8

P
patterns 8
pence (p) 29
place value 3
position 37
pounds (£) 29
pyramids 36

Q
quarter full 27
quarter turn 38
quarters 21
quicker 33

R
rectangles 35
ruler 24

S
scales 26
second place 8
seconds 33
shapes 35, 36
    2D shapes 35
    3D shapes 36
sharing 18
short 23
slower 33
spheres 36
squares 35
subtracting 12, 14, 15

T
tall 23, 24
tens 3
third place 8
three-quarter turn 38
time 32, 33
today 31
tomorrow 31
triangles 35
turns 38

V
volume 27, 28

W
weeks 30
weight 25, 26
whole turn 38

Y
year 30
yesterday 31

Z
zero 15